HAPPY OUTDOORS

HAPPY OUTDOORS

*A Collection of Stories
from the Woods and Water*

Clifford J. Ray III

XULON PRESS

Xulon Press
2301 Lucien Way #415
Maitland, FL 32751
407.339.4217
www.xulonpress.com

Unless otherwise indicated, Unless otherwise indicated, Bible
quotations are taken from the New Living Translation, copyright
1996, 2004, 2007 by the Tyndale House Foundation.

Paperback ISBN-13: 978-1-6628-1853-0
Ebook ISBN-13: 978-1-6628-1854-7

DEDICATION

For my two boys

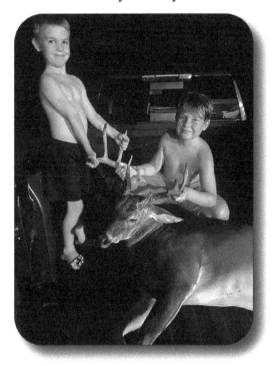

Jace (age 7) and Harrison (age 11)

Acknowledgements

I would like to thank Ben Buchanan and Kaitlin Courtnay for their proofreading and helpful advice.

TABLE OF CONTENTS

Dedication v

Acknowledgements vii

Introduction xi

Chapter 1: World's First 1

Chapter 2: Outdoor Moments 9

Chapter 3: Monsters 19

Chapter 4: Angry Fish 25

Chapter 5: Rendezvous with Destiny 29

Chapter 6: Key Largo, OHIO 35

Chapter 7: Southern Whitetail Guide Service 43

Chapter 8: Chemo Buck 51

Chapter 9: Toughness 55

Chapter 10: Deer Gets Hunter 63

Chapter 11: Fishing Electricity 71

Chapter 12: Second Chance 77

Chapter 13: Bucknell Football 2018 87

Chapter 14: Mean Dean 93

Conclusion 99

About the Author 103

INTRODUCTION

I n March of 2017, I met Captain Rick Percy from Beaufort, South Carolina. Captain Rick operates a fishing charter service. We fished together one cold spring morning. Not long into our trip, fishing stories became the hot topic. I listened most of the time, trying to pick up wisdom from a man who fishes nearly 300 days per year. Eventually, a few of my tales were able to hold serve. As usual I talked a little about my cancer journey, writing my first book, and fishing around Edisto Island. He couldn't believe I was a cancer survivor. I look healthy now, but back in 2011 my body was pretty weak. After listening to many of his stories, I said to Rick, "You need to write a book. How neat would it be to give a customer of yours a book after a charter?" He said the thought had never crossed his mind, but I could tell a fire had been lit.

After less than a year, Captain Rick mailed me his book straight off the press. He gives me too much of the credit for his accomplishment; all I did was notice his potential and point him in the right direction. Captain Rick made it happen.

Over the past few months, Captain Rick has been in my thoughts quite often. He called me back in August (2020) to let me know he was diagnosed with thyroid cancer. It's always a sickening feeling for me when I hear of someone being diagnosed. I know it's a long journey to being healthy, and a type of misery that's only completely understood by the patient. We talked for a while, and I let him know that I would add him to our church prayer list. I pray for Captain Rick's recovery quite often.

After hearing the news, I pulled out Rick's book and started reading it again. I can hear his voice telling the stories as I read them. A realization of how special this book is flooded my thoughts, especially what it must mean for his family. In the introduction, he mentioned how he hoped his daughters could pick up the book after he's gone and feel his presence with them. I hope that's one day far in the future. Captain Rick has a lot more fish to catch!

Well, guess what? After putting Captain Rick's book down, I started thumbing through my first two books. I quickly realized that it's priceless having these books. As the years pass, it's amazing how we forget so many of the details. It's like losing some of the smiles and joy that add meaning to life. The turn of each page brings back to life lost memories.

A few weeks after talking with Rick, the wheels of motivation began to spin for me once again. The fire to complete my third book was rekindled. The busyness of life just makes it hard to find time to write. However, the slowdown of 2020 offered me the window of opportunity that I needed.

Since the government wanted us to avoid people this year, I hunted more than ever. This time in the woods was rejuvenating. It was the water and sunshine to a dormant seed that was working hard to sprout. Over several hunts, my mind couldn't shake the idea of completing the third book. I began it back in 2018, but the desire fizzled out. I kept thinking: *Do I have enough in the story tank to complete this book... an outdoor book filled with hunting and fishing stories? I started this project two years ago, and for whatever reason, I lost my enthusiasm and energy to write. I need to finish what I started.*

Just so you know, the dormant seed I'm referring to was planted on a fall fishing trip back in 2018. It's neat how within the matter of a few minutes an idea can be born. When I know: *this needs to be a story for another book one day.* Well, you can imagine how happy I was when the initial idea for this book was born. It was slowly building over sixteen years, while operating both my hunting and fishing guide services. Then, on one of my last charters, many chapters for this book began to fall into place. All it took was a bag of chocolate chip cookies and some cold beer to bring everything together.

I remember the exact moment when the first thought for this book was conceived. On that special fall trip in 2018, my buddy and I were in a dry spell. Nothing was biting, not even the sand gnats. At this time, I began rattling off a few stories. I could tell my friend was truly engrossed. During story time, we polished off several cold ones, and he ate a sack full of chocolate chip cookies. I told him those cookies were addictive and he proved me correct. Well, after about the third story he looked at me with all seriousness and said, "I'll tell you what... there are a lot of boring people in this world, but you sure as hell ain't one of them!"

I laughed and responded, "You know what? I haven't even scratched the surface." I took what he said as a compliment and his honesty was well received.

My friend's straight forward statement, which was possibly alcohol induced, was encouraging to me. The need to write a book filled with some of my favorite tales became a new goal to accomplish. Over the years, I have discovered the memories that last have little to do with how many fish were caught. It's the unexpected moments that make the best stories. A good story typically stretches the boundary of truth. However, it's really special when a seemingly far-fetched story is totally true! Those are the ones I love to tell.

Life has many ebbs and flows or up and downs. Thankfully, my vigor for writing returned this year while hunting. This book may have one story in it that brings a smile to someone's face during a tough time. If that's the best result I can get, then it's worth it to me. You know why? I have been in that bad moment (fighting cancer) when a smile was a million miles away. This book is the result of perseverance or in other words: "getting through the tough times." It's my way of doing something positive.

Happy Outdoors is a gift to my two boys. I write because, in the back of my mind, cancer can come unannounced. Ten years ago, I was blindsided with Hodgkin's Lymphoma. During the journey, I was warned of a potential secondary cancer. I know life can be rudely interrupted at any moment. Just two hours ago, another skin cancer surgery was performed on my back. It was nothing major, however, nine stiches were needed to close the area. Cancer loves me for whatever reason.

I have done my best to make my personal stories interesting for everyone to read. People who know my family may find the book more interesting than others. I understand that. Also, if hunting and fishing aren't a part of your life, then you definitely need to find another book. I'm just being honest. Finally, while reading, you'll see that the stories do not follow any type of chronological order. The first three chapters bring you up to speed on our family's lifelong connection to the outdoors; after that, the majority of the book is filled with hunting and fishing stories. The final two chapters are surprises. I hope this helps you understand the book a little better. One more thing: I have always been happy outdoors, and that's why I chose this title.

I intended to end the introduction with the paragraph above, which was written a couple of months ago. However, life doesn't have a pause button.

January 23, 2021 (Sunday)

Captain Rick's fishing website isn't available. I wonder why? That's what the computer kept telling me. Something just isn't right. Since meeting Rick four years ago, the site has been online 100% of the time. His fishing reports are second to none. Reading the reports keeps me in the loop with Rick and the fishing activity around Beaufort. Also, Captain Rick would periodically post an update on his health. On this morning, that's what I was looking for; the fishing report page evolved into a health report page. I was hoping to read some good news and see a picture of him fishing with a buddy. Today was different.

Yes, I saw a picture and discovered sad news, but it wasn't on his site. After some searching, I found my answer. Captain Rick lost his battle with cancer. His obituary read, "He passed away in his sleep on Thursday, January 14, 2021, at the Beaufort Memorial Hospital after a tough fight with anaplastic thyroid cancer." The obituary continued, "His energy and enthusiasm for the outdoors was infectious! He got so excited for every cast or shot by anyone lucky enough to be with him." I was one of those lucky people. When you love what you are doing, it shows. It was an honor to call Captain Rick a friend. He was one of the best fishermen ever to fish on the coast of South Carolina.

WORLD'S FIRST

C ommercial fishing was a part of our family for twenty-two years. C.J. Ray, Jr., (my father) ran two different operations. He shrimped out of Bennett's Point, which is near Edisto Beach, and fished for the American shad on the Savannah River near Millet, SC. The shrimping stories are too much in the past for me to accurately write about. The boat was sold just after I was born. However, I was a part of the shad fishing business for about eight years. Meaning, I was a witness to the operation. It was a business that was far from the ordinary. Stories that may seem unrealistic or far-fetched were normal operations. This story is a perfect example. My boys need to know this one.

Most likely you may be unfamiliar with commercial shad fishing, so here's a quick lesson to get started. The season for the American shad in the Savannah River runs from January first through the end of April. The shad is a species of anadromous fish. This just means they spend most of their lives in saltwater and then spawn in freshwater. A typical shad is between four to six pounds. Females are larger than the males. Gill set nets are one way to catch these fish, and this was our method of choice. They swim headfirst through the webbing of the net and then become entangled as they try to free themselves. The fish caught in the net were removed daily and placed in coolers packed full of ice. Once enough fish were caught, we would sell them to various fish markets. As you can imagine, numerous species of fish were caught. Following shad, the most common were: catfish, buffalo, carp, and gar fish.

Well, this story revolves around another species that was accidentally caught: the federally endangered shortnose sturgeon. Since these fish were federally protected, they had to be released unharmed. Sturgeon are tough, pre-historic fish and can handle being caught up in the net for hours.

During the 1984 shad season, federal biologists were interested in this fish. They needed the sturgeon for a spawning project. However, catching the fish didn't come easily for them. One day on the river, they ran across C.J. and struck up a conversation. The rest is history, as they say. The article below was written by Mr. Pete Laurie in June of 1984. It was published in *The State* newspaper in July of 1984. I reread it a few months ago and realized something that was actually amazing. See if you have the same conclusion after reading the article. As an eight-year old, I helped release the first ever artificially spawned sturgeon back into the wild. So, if I'm correct, C.J.

and I were the first people in the world to do this. Sounds pretty amazing, doesn't it? I simply rewrote the article below because it would be too difficult to read from the original newspaper print.

> Savannah River: One thousand juvenile shortnose sturgeon were released here in early June by C.J. Ray, Jr., the same commercial fisherman who had helped capture the parents of the endangered fish months earlier from the same area.

> The two-inch long juvenile fish had been spawned in captivity, the first ever successful artificial spawning of shortnose sturgeon, as part of a project to develop culture techniques for both the shortnose and the commercially important Atlantic sturgeon.

> The sturgeon project is a cooperative effort of the South Carolina Wildlife and Marine Resources Department and the U.S. Fish and Wildlife Service (USFWS).

Ray, a commercial shad fisherman from nearby Denmark, S.C., worked closely with scientists from the state and federal agencies.

Although endangered species laws require short-nose sturgeon caught in commercial fishing gear be released immediately, Ray was given special permission to hold the sturgeon captured accidentally.

He placed the fish in special floating pens and notified researchers who transported them to the USFWS's Orangeburg National Fish Hatchery.

"It was a lot of work but I loved doing it," Ray said.

An 8.5-pound female and an 8-pound male spawned successfully on April 10. After a five-day incubation period 5,500 eggs were hatched through the efforts of Rodney Lindsey, a biologist at the Orangeburg Hatchery.

According to Dr. Ted Smith of the Marine Resources Division, siblings of the fish released are being reared in both state and federal facilities.

"Studies are being conducted to provide information on growth rates, diets, survival rates and optimal environmental conditions," Smith said. "This will be a long term undertaking as there are still many things we need to determine before we can routinely stock small juvenile sturgeon and expect them to grow to maturity," Smith noted.

If successful, such techniques could be used to restock and rehabilitate native populations along the entire east coast, Smith said.

The shortnose sturgeon is a much smaller species with mature fish only weighing eight pounds while mature Atlantic sturgeon weigh 100-400 lbs.

Several years earlier, Smith and Ted Dingley, manager of the Orangeburg hatchery and co-investigator in the project, were the first to successfully spawn the much larger Atlantic sturgeon in captivity. Again, they worked in conjunction with commercial fisherman to obtain brood stock.

Smith said, "The caviar and flesh from the Atlantic sturgeon is highly prized; however, the commercial fishery in South Carolina has suffered drastic declines in recent years. This once abundant fish is now greatly reduced in numbers." The shortnose sturgeon was once harvested commercially in South Carolina, but this species was declared endangered by the federal government in 1972. If work goes as planned, the scientist hoped to demonstrate large-scale techniques for producing Atlantic coast sturgeon over the next several years.

"We greatly appreciate the assistance of Mr. Ray in obtaining the adult sturgeon. We felt he should have the honor of releasing the first batch of hatchery produced juveniles into their native river," the scientist said.

Releasing Sturgeon Fingerlings into the Savannah River

THE OUTDOOR CHANNEL

At the age of twenty-four, I began the process of creating a deer hunting service from scratch. This just seemed like a natural step for me. Hunting has always been a part of my life. I even majored in wildlife biology at Clemson. How could I not give this a try?

Basically, all of the big-ticket items were already in place. Our family owned all the land where we would hunt. Our livelihood was farming, so maintaining food plots was right up our alley. I gathered valuable information from a few local guides and took advice from experienced outdoorsmen. Months of planning and hard work finally came together a year later, when Southern Whitetail Guide Service began operating in August of 2001.

My very first hunters were from the Washington, D.C. area. It always amazed me how far people would travel to hunt for a day or two. One of my favorite groups came all the way from Harrisburg, Pennsylvania. They made the trip three consecutive years.

For nine years, the doors were open to hunters across America. However, my niche served the east coast. During the first few years of operation, I was aggressive in trying to reach hunters. Day and night, my mind was constantly dialed into growing the service. Well, this attitude led me on a unique journey. Very few people know any of the details of what I'm about to share. The story is too long to tell in person… not only that, but it simply seems too fictional. However, it happened. I managed to pull defeat from the jaws of victory. That's correct. I gave it my best—let's just leave it at that!

The Outdoor Channel was more than just a TV network when I was a young hunting businessman. I watched religiously for ideas to grow the service. In 2002, during my second year of operation, *Carolina Outdoors* caught my eye. This show was based in South Carolina and seemed to be down to earth. I enjoyed that characteristic about the show, and each passing episode piqued my interest more and more. Soon, the wheels inside my young mind started spinning. *This is it,* I thought. *I need these fellows to hunt with me for one show. That'll put me on the map.* I remember jotting down the producer's name as one episode concluded.

Weeks passed as I contemplated my next move. *How in the world am I going to pull this off?* Then the answer to the mystery became obvious. As one show was about to end, the host informed viewers about an upcoming striper tournament on Clarks Hill. Anyone interested could be a part of the weigh in at the boat landing. My prayers had been answered.

I arrived early on tournament day. This was on a cold Saturday in December. The host was already at the landing, preparing for the day. Immediately, I introduced myself and shared the purpose for my visit. We talked for a while, and soon the producer's phone number was in my pocket. The plan was coming together.

Monday morning couldn't arrive fast enough. I called the producer (Robert) bright and early. I'm an early bird, in case you don't know. Robert and I had a good conversation. He eventually invited me to Florence, where *Carolina Outdoors* was produced. Within a few days, I was sitting in his office. The dream was one step closer.

We talked for an hour like old friends. He was funny and full of energy, a loud talker with plenty of jokes. I was practically a family member after our meeting. He lined me up with another show called *Outdoor Moments*. I can't recall the reason why, but it didn't matter. I just wanted a deer hunting show during the rut. He could tell I was a man on a mission.

I'm one heck of a salesman! I thought to myself. *Twenty-six years old and about to showcase my service on television.* This was my opportunity to show the nation how good our deer hunting was. Once this show aired, I was on my way to becoming somebody in the deer hunting industry. Robert even mentioned the annual Shot Show Conference during our meeting. This is where all the hunting bigwigs rubbed elbows. *Holy cow! I might be there next year!* Yes, that thought crossed my mind.

Driving home, I was so happy. I did it! The crew from *Outdoor Moments* was soon to be filming on our property. The hunt was just around the corner, too. Our turkey season begins March fifteenth, and the crew was eager to get an early season bird.

What in the hell just happened? How did I agree to this? How did I go from deer hunting to turkeys? I never wanted a turkey hunting show! My plan crumbled during the old friend's reunion. The producer fast-talked me (in a positive way), and I caved to his needs. They needed a turkey show and I agreed. *Well, I better pull out the turkey calls.*

My excitement grew for the upcoming turkey hunt. The days passed like molasses until finally our hunting weekend arrived. The crew arrived at one of our local motels around 8:00 PM Friday night. After getting settled in, the host gave me a call. It was exciting to talk to him on the phone. I immediately drove to the motel to welcome him and plan our day. It was really happening! Months of planning and dreaming was soon to be a reality.

Sadly, Saturday morning's excitement slowly turned into Saturday afternoon's disappointment. We hunted all day long and only saw one hen. The T.V. hunt quickly turned into a failure. The host promised he would send his co-host another weekend to try one more time. That was a welcomed spirit boost. However, I'm sure my feelings of disgust were easy to see.

Well, hunt number two turned out to be exactly like hunt number one. We hunted all day long and saw absolutely nothing. I'm sure this crew was losing confidence in me pretty fast. Everything we tried failed; not a single gobble all day long. We collectively agreed our turkey hunting adventure just wasn't panning out. I just knew the dream was over. Too my surprise, our focus quickly shifted to the upcoming deer season. The host informed me that they really wanted to get a buck in velvet on film. Of course, I was all in on the velvet hunt in August, even though this was not my original plan. Our property turns into deer heaven during the rut—not in August when it's ninety-five degrees! Why do I keep wavering from what I know works? I just had my fingers crossed something positive would happen.

May 25th, 2003

To: Dean and Lisa Ray
Southern Whitetail Guide Service

Bub, Kelly, and I would like to thank you both again for inviting us back for some great spring turkey action at *Southern Whitetail Guide Service* this past spring. As always, the *Outdoor Moments* film crew experienced great hunting, as well as "True Southern Hospitality". It has not only been a great pleasure to meet you both, but also for the friendships we have created to share in the future.

Keep up the good work, and may God continue to bless *Southern Whitetail Guide Service* and all others who come to visit you.

We wish you both much success this 2003 season and look forward to some awesome *"Buck in Velvet"* deer hunting action!

Sincerely,

A Letter from the Outdoor Moments Crew

I'm not going to beat around the bush. The August hunting turned out exactly like I thought it would. We basically saw nothing. Only a few small bucks over three weekends. It was flat-out awful.

Collectively, we all agreed to move on. It just wasn't working out. They needed kills, and my focus shifted to running the service. The rut was approaching, and my weekends were about to become busy with deer hunters.

Like always, when the rut was in full swing, we started dropping bucks. Had I stuck to the original plan, I know for certain things would have turned out better. I was just too young to stick to my guns.

This failure didn't sit well with me. I blew it with one hunting show; maybe something else would surface. There were several shows based in the southeast that I could line up and give it another go.

Four years later (2007), I was sitting in the production office of another outdoor television show. This time I was in Rock Hill, home town of *Huntin' the World Southern Style*. I just don't give up easy. The co-host (Ken) and I met for over an hour, talking and planning a trip. He was just as funny as the first producer in Florence. We hit it off immediately. Just like before, my plan was to film a deer hunting show during the rut which is the best time of year to hunt in Denmark! Once all of the dust had settled, everything was set. Our calendars were marked for a redfish fishing show in Beaufort, SC. I swear I can't make this stuff up. *How in the hell did this happen a second time?*

I actually have the answer. We started talking about fishing, and I mentioned my intentions of running a charter business. Well, one thing led to another, and the next thing you knew the trip was planned. This was years before my intended starting date. The opportunity presented itself and I jumped on it.

Believe it or not, we had a fun day on the water. Ken and I caught about fifteen redfish. There was one problem, though. The fish were all small. Everything was around thirteen inches. We did catch one that stretched the tape to twenty-three inches, but we just didn't have enough quality for a show.

Just like with *Outdoor Moments*, this crew promised to fish with me again. I should have learned my lesson from the turkey hunts in 2003. We fished two more times, and were skunked on both trips. Why couldn't I make this work? It was just weird how things turned out. I felt like I was trying to beat a square peg into a round slot. It seemed like no matter what I did, nothing worked.

Two failures were enough for me. The lesson was learned. I decided to keep my hunting service at a level that I could maintain. To be honest, both the hunting and eventual fishing charter business were nothing more than serious hobbies. Looking back, I truly believe had the shows been successful, they would have put too much strain on my life. Saturdays and Sundays would have just become another day of work. All of my free time would have been consumed maintaining both services. I was chasing a dream that was a dead end. Of course, I didn't think of it that way back then; you see, no children were in the picture. I could come and go as I pleased. As you all know, priorities and goals change when a couple of little boys are running around. Family soon became my full-time priority. Someone above was pulling the reigns back on me. I did my best to break loose. The harder I tried, the more I failed. My plans were being shut down for a different purpose.

MONSTERS

As a young boy, walking to the deer stand early in the morning was nerve wracking. My favorite stand was located about a half-mile behind our house. In order to get there, I walked across an open cow pasture that eventually led to the hardwoods. You can't imagine the monsters I saw crossing that field. Not only did I see them, but a few chased me! Moonlight turns every tree and bush into something about to attack! After successfully crossing the field, it was time to enter the dark hardwoods. Now, this is where the Bogeyman lived. Many times, I ran as fast as possible to get to my stand. I figured if he was going to get me he had to be fast. Flashlight, rifle, and knife were all my potential tools for battle if needed. Time after time, I always made it to my stand. I'm not sure why, but the stand was a safe haven. All fears eased away once the .270 was loaded. Trust me—had Bigfoot, Godzilla, the Bogeyman, or any of their buddies walked out on me, they wouldn't live to scare another little boy!

The make-believe monsters really worked on my mental health as a new hunter. Even nowadays, a covey of quail or a deer jumping up nearby will get the heart pumping. Those moments always bring back thoughts of the evil creatures that were lurking in the woods. Well, I'm here to let you know there is one creature hiding in the woods that'll make every hunter squeal like a little girl. We all have a story about this hidden devil. Isn't it ironic that the real animal I needed to fear never crossed my mind as a little boy?

Our deer season in Bamberg County starts on August 15th. Hunting in August is miserable, in my opinion. I leave that to young boys and people from out of state that don't know any better. It's simply too hot. However, while operating my hunting service in the 2000s, one detail of the job was to pre- pare the stands before opening day. I enjoyed the work and the heat was never an issue. It's just part of growing up in South Carolina. Summer work attire consisted of shorts, a hat, and boots. Bug spray was my shirt. I also needed very few tools to get a stand ready for the upcoming year. You see, stands are seldom moved once in place. Our hunting spots are pretty much set. So typically, the tools of the day were simple: wasp spray, a saw, string, and new camouflage covering. A stand could be completely camouflaged and ready to hunt in about thirty minutes.

One particular stand will always bring back memories. I noticed a nail that needed to be hammered back into the tree.

This meant heading back to the truck to get a hammer. The truck was located about one hundred yards through the hardwoods. I was in a hurry to finish up so I ran back to the truck. Thank goodness, today I was wearing my tennis shoes. I could move through the woods better than Bo Jackson on a football field. After grabbing the hammer, I started back to the stand. While sprinting to the stand, a small patch of briars blocked my path. I quickly decided to test my hurdling ability so I picked up speed and launched myself over the briars. The briars were cleared, and now the focus shifted to the landing. Looking toward the ground, my eyes focused on the worst sight I have ever seen (my skin is crawling as I write this).

A rattlesnake was coiled up at the exact point of my landing. To this day, I don't know how I didn't land on top of him. My heel landed just inches from his body. Phantom fangs paralyzed my thoughts. Mentally, I could feel them buried in my calf. There's little doubt that a world record triple jump took place escaping the viper. Once a safe distance away, I turned around to face a real monster. I soon came face-to-face with a canebrake rattlesnake.

I positioned myself safely out of his sight to plan my next move. It was time to kill. I hit him as hard as possible with a stick. After the whap, his head raised up a few inches and he simply looked at me. I really don't think I phased him at all.

Now, he's pissed and I'm on his radar! Only a second passed by before I popped him again. This time it was lights out. He was graveyard dead!

Walking through the woods became extremely difficult. It was like I was walking in a mine field. My Bo Jackson pace turned into grandmama mode. When I reached the truck, I stretched my unwanted prize across the tailgate. This is when it became apparent why he wasn't interested in striking. His belly was full. He had just killed and eaten. It looked as if he had a softball in his stomach. Man, I was lucky on this day. That's the real monster all hunters need to respect. Bigfoot ain't got nothin' on a rattlesnake!

The close call rattlesnake

ANGRY FISH

T he boat landing separates real fishermen from green horns. Backing a boat into the water doesn't come naturally for some people. This task can be a comedy of errors and typically brings out the worst in many people. Maybe my skills seem better than the average Joe; I have been asked to load boats, back the trailer, and park trucks with trailers on numerous occasions. I gladly help in these situations and have probably saved a few marriages in the process. More times than not it's a lady who asks for my assistance while their husband is in the boat. However, there's one man out there who may have a bounty on me still to this day. Here's the story from my point of view. I sure don't care for his!

The day was almost over, in my opinion. The boat was tied up at the landing, and I was backing my trailer into the water to load the boat. That's when business picked up and my peaceful day turned sour. As soon as I got out of my truck, I heard a man yelling at the top of his lungs from his boat. He was a short distance out from the landing as his buddy backed the trailer down the ramp. I looked around to see what in the world was going on. I made eye contact with the man on the boat and he was pointing directly at me. "I'm going to kill you!" was the only sentence he could say. Trust me, I heard him loud and clear because he said it about a dozen times. I have never seen someone that angry in my life. I'm telling you, my mind kicked into high gear. *What in the world did I do?*

Realizing this fellow looked like Goliath and that he had a tag team partner if needed, I was in a bad situation. So, I pulled my truck out of the water several feet just in case I needed to break camp really fast. His buddy looked as calm as a cucumber while backing the trailer into the water. I approached him as calmly as possible. Seeing as I was about to be killed, I felt like I needed to know what I had done. I asked Goliath's buddy, "What in the world did I do?"

He replied, "He's pissed because you cut us off out there on the water."

I told him I was sorry for that, and stated that I didn't even see his boat. I thought Goliath was either drunk or on drugs because no one in their right mind could get this angry. That's really what was scaring me about my current predicament.

Goliath saw me talking to his buddy and decided he wanted to kill me because I was near his truck. "Get the hell away from my truck or I'm going to kill you!"

To be honest, I really didn't know what to do. I walked to the front of my truck and leaned on the hood, watching a mad man load his boat on the trailer. At the same time, he was yelling and throwing mullet, squid, and every piece of bait he had on my boat. I just watched hoping he didn't shoot me. He finally loaded his boat and his buddy pulled him up on the hill. He yelled and pointed his fingers at me the whole time. As soon as he passed me, I backed my trailer into the water and loaded my boat in record time. I pulled out of the water and put several football fields in between me and Goliath. In no time, my boat was tied down and I was off. Still to this day, I can't figure out how or if I really cut them off. I am a defensive boat driver. I always give way or slow down way before time. There are so many fools on the water you have to constantly be on the look-out. Obviously, I made a mistake on this day in someone's opinion. Thank goodness I survived to share the story.

PS: I have seen his truck one other time at the landing. I thought about cutting all four of his tires, but I figured I'd better not stir the pot.

RENDEZVOUS WITH DESTINY

I t'll probably snow in Jamaica before I catch a tarpon. Nope, you know what? Carolina will beat Clemson in football. Well, we all know that's not going to happen anytime soon. Currently, the streak is at six straight loses and counting! As long as Dabo's around, Clemson ain't losing.

Okay, I'm getting off subject. Let's get back to fishing.

It's a sad fact that I have struggled for years to catch one of these big fish. I don't think I'm all alone in this category, but it just feels like I'm snakebit. Many guides are satisfied with a single hook-up per trip. Once hooked, getting one to the boat is another big challenge. They are masters at throwing the hook. I wish I knew this from experience. However, it's just what I have been told.

These past two seasons, I have fished more than ever for tarpon with absolutely nothing to show for my efforts except sunburns and skin cancer scars. It's awfully hot on our coast in August. I don't mind enduring the blistering sun if that is what it takes. "No guts, no glory," as the saying goes.

Listen, I may be a little hard-nosed when dealing with our blistering sun, but I'm openminded when it comes to learning from local fishing guides. I'm not shy to ask questions. A few years ago, I talked with a guide who fishes for tarpon regularly. We both happened to be fishing in a redfish tournament in Beaufort. I asked him how his tarpon season went. He was very proud to inform me he had nine hook-ups and landed four. To be honest, I thought that was absolutely incredible. Another buddy of mine is also a guide in Beaufort; he typically catches about five per season as well. So, you can see, this fish is tough to catch.

This is where "Rendezvous with Destiny" begins. This tale resembles fiction more than reality. What happened on September 29, 2017, has to go down as one of the best South Carolina fishing stories of all time. I'm not making that up either. Michael, Cholly, Bryce, and C.J. hit the jack pot. Their day started out with anticipation of catching a few bull reds in the Port Royal Sound just off Hilton Head. As it turned out, they tapped into the tarpon treasure box.

The details of the day were passed along to me by Cholly just after the Pelion High School football game. You see, Cholly was lucky he didn't miss the trip. He was actually supposed to be on the radio that Friday night. Cholly was the football summary voice for the Pelion High School football team. His job was to contact *The Game* radio show at the end of each quarter to give updates. Thursday night he called me and asked if I would like to fill in for the radio assignment. I eagerly said yes and was very happy to fill in. I also knew my son (Harrison) would love sitting in the press box during the football game. It was a win-win for all.

It was win-win until about 10:15 PM Friday night. This is when I received the phone call that would change tarpon fishing forever. Cholly called and I immediately knew something big time had happened. He was laughing on the other end, "You're not going to believe what happened today!" I couldn't wait to hear the news. He continued, "I'm not kidding you, and I have witnesses. We hooked eleven tarpon and landed three today."

I was in absolute shock. I couldn't believe it. All I could say was, "How?"

"We even had two doubles," Cholly stated.

"How in the world did you do that?" I was still stunned to say the least.

"We fished the same spot as we did last year for bull reds and this time it was full of tarpon," Cholly replied. By this point, he started filling me in with the details of the day and it was amazing. However, eleven and three was all my mind could focus on. Everyone involved, including me, has agreed not to ever mention this story to anyone who fishes for tarpon. Who would believe eleven of these giants could possibly be hooked in five hours? No one who actually fishes for them in South Carolina.

Isn't it ironic that this snake-bit tarpon fisherman has been given the opportunity to share this tale? Three of my good friends and my own daddy accomplished something that I could only dream about. Shoot, I would like to catch just one! This incredible fishing day might just be the best tarpon trip in the history of South Carolina. Of course, this is a self-proclaimed title. However, most tarpon fisherman can't produce results like this for an entire season.

Bryce, Michael, & C.J. with a big Tarpon

KEY LARGO, OHIO

During my Outdoor Channel fanatic phase, Monday nights won hands down, because two straight hours of saltwater fishing came on during prime time. *Mark Sosin's Saltwater Journal* kicked off the night followed by more fantastic fishing shows. Many of Sosin's shows were filmed in Florida. He had me hook, line, and sinker during those episodes. I even convinced myself that I could catch a bone fish in the Florida Keys. It didn't look that hard from my couch.

I decided to fish out of Key Largo, Florida, in the summer of 2005. This was going to be fun. One of my goals was to meet some of the salty fisherman and, of course, people like Jimmy Buffet. Everyone in the Keys has to be like Buffet. You know what I'm talking about; the locals that grew up in the Keys. Also, the trip needed to be done as cheaply as possible. A budget was in place. So, during my planning stage, I decided to stay two nights at the local campground to save some money.

Just south of Miami, on day two of traveling, I pulled into a bait and tackle store to purchase my Florida fishing license. During the transaction, the store clerk looked at my driver's license. He saw my hometown was Denmark, SC. To my surprise, he mentioned his father lived in North, SC. That blew me away because North is about twenty minutes from Denmark. It's a small world. I'm in Miami meeting someone who knows about North and Denmark!

After purchasing the license, I wasted no time on the way to Key Largo. I could hear the fish calling my name. Priority number one was to locate the camp site. This was accomplished rather easily. I spoke with the guard at the entrance and informed her of my intentions.

Before we go any further in this story, I need to explain something. At this point in my life, I seldom ventured out of Denmark or the neighboring small towns on my own. Denmark has three stop lights. It was a big deal when we got a McDonald's. I could buy beer and cigarettes at ten-years old for workers on our family farm. The store owners knew me. My point being, I'm from a small town and have always played by a different set of rules than most people. My real-world lessons were about to begin in Florida (at twenty-nine years old).

The guard informed me that the camp site needed a twenty-four-hour notice for visitors. I'm sure she saw the disgust on my face. I then informed her that I had just driven eleven hours over two days and really needed some lenience on the notification rule. She wouldn't budge on the rule. She really pissed me off, to say the least. Obviously, she didn't know who I was or where I was from. Now, my budget was about to be blown! I had to waste money on a motel room. Well, I drove up and down Highway 1 looking for a decent, cheap place to stay. I also needed a motel with a big parking lot for my boat. It didn't take long to find a nice place. I parked the truck and went inside to book a room for two nights. The lady at the front desk started typing on the computer and said, "That's going to be five hundred." I didn't even give her time to finish. I ran out of that place and never looked back.

What in the hell am I going to do now? All right, it's time to stay calm, I thought to myself. *I reckon I've got to lower my standards for a place to stay.* I hopped back in the truck and drove around some more. I finally found an old rundown place that looked semi-reasonable. I was scared to ask the price, to be honest with you. Thank goodness, the price was within my range at one-hundred and twenty dollars a night. I booked a room for two nights. Then I asked the second most important question: "Do you have room enough for me to park my boat?" The woman assured me there was plenty of room for the boat. All right, we were getting somewhere.

Finally, feeling somewhat comfortable in Key Largo, I asked the lady where she was from. To my disappointment, she was from Ohio. "Ohio!" I responded. After a little more investigating on my part, I found out most of the people around me were from the North. No, not North, SC, but real northerners (Yankees). I'm thinking to myself, *What in the world*? I came down here to meet some Florida Key locals and I somehow found myself in the middle of Ohio. The light bulb is going off that this place isn't what I had envisioned. Jimmy Buffet and Mark Sosin had screwed me. Guess what? Buffet is from Alabama!

Well, it was too late now; the room was booked and it was time to fish. I just needed to unpack and find a good parking place for the boat. Well, another rude awakening was about to be exposed. There's not a damn parking spot big enough for a moped on this property! I finally went back into the motel office and explained my dilemma. She picked a fine time to inform me that I could just park on the curb by the highway. I had absolutely had it with this place. I cared too much about my truck and boat to park on the curb of the main highway. I asked her as nicely as possible to give me my money back. I was going home! She said she couldn't do that. My blood was boiling now, and I could eat nails! Somehow, I kept my cool at the front desk. I finally said, "Give me one night's money back and you can have the second. I just don't care anymore." I finally won a battle (I think) because she agreed. To be honest, I couldn't think straight anymore. The Yankees had won again.

While leaving the office, one nice fellow (from Ohio) tried to convince me not to leave. We'd talked earlier and he knew I had just arrived from South Carolina. I wasn't hearing anything he said, however, he did convince me to fish a little while before leaving. So, around five o'clock I launched my boat from the motel landing. Finally, I found a little peace as I made way through the mangroves. Knowing very little about fishing in the Keys, I started throwing a top water plug. I fished about thirty minutes and had two bites. In hindsight, the bites were probably snapper. I'll explain that in a second. I spent about two hours on the water and decided to call it a day. The eleven-hour drive home was going to be tough. I loaded the boat up and hauled tail back home. My head lights finally crossed the South Carolina state line at approximately four AM. That was one of the most miserable experiences and drives of my life to say the least. I promised myself to never go back to the Keys. I'm done with those Florida Yankees.

Time does heal misery. In 2010, just five years after my fiasco, my wife decided to attend a work conference in Key West. I went and used a little common sense this time around. I booked a fishing guide out of Islamorada. I had the best time and caught two big permit, a barracuda, and several other fish (including snapper). The guide said snapper were everywhere, so that's how I figured out I probably got snapper bites on my previous trip.

I very seldom tell this story. It' just too much to explain and almost unbelievable. However, I learned a couple valuable lessons. Among them: pay for a guide when fishing areas that are unfamiliar. Finally, I love fishing in South Carolina and will not take my boat across the state line again. This trip broke the horse's back!

31-pound Islamorada Permit

SOUTHERN WHITETAIL
GUIDE SERVICE

N ine years was plenty. The energy and motivation needed to guide hunters had simply faded. My heart just wasn't in it anymore. As the years passed, the service slowly turned into a job. The fun was gone.

The last hunter, like the first, was from Washington D.C. On the final hunt in late December (2009), my guest shot a nice six point. I remember dragging the buck out of the woods and thinking to myself: *I'm done*. The time had come to close the service, and just like that, this chapter of my life was over.

Operating the service was an awful lot of work and a time-consuming endeavor. However, at this time in my life I had plenty of free time. Children were not even on the radar yet. More importantly, I needed a challenge at this point in my life. My day job just wasn't doing it for me. Life seemed stagnant and boring, a feeling that was unfamiliar and uneasy. I was twenty-four years old and needed to test myself. This service was the answer.

I may have made a small amount of money, but it was never about the money. My internal fire was being satisfied. I really enjoyed meeting hunters from all along the east coast. It was also really neat to hear honest comments from hunters throughout their stay. Things like: *I have never seen that many deer; I can't believe I killed two in the same hunt; that's the biggest buck I have ever killed*; or *we are definitely coming back next year.* You could tell they were sincerely happy. Their comments were my reward. Just so you know, I purposely tried to forget any of the negative words. I was well aware that you can't satisfy everyone. There were a few hunters that caused me to second guess the need to be in business. However, after all of the dust had settled, it was a great nine years.

In my mind, pictures are the best way to give an account of the service. Countless guests, friends, and family members have benefitted from our hunting property. Here are a few of the bucks that have put smiles on people's faces.

SLOW MODE HUNTING

I t was twenty-seven degrees when I sat down this morning; that's cold for South Carolina deer hunting. To be honest, I was in low gear today. My goal was to just watch and observe. Nine stitches are in my back from Wednesday's skin cancer surgery. I know it isn't a lot. However, per doctor's orders, I'm not supposed to lift anything heavy for a few days. Yes, an exception would have been made if a big one crossed my path. Stitches could be repaired if necessary.

It probably sounds strange for someone to go hunting and have zero intention of picking up the gun, but sitting in the woods alone is time well spent in my opinion. It's peaceful. Actually, this morning I spent a lot of time thinking about this story. When was the last time I went hunting and just watched? There is one hunt that overshadows all the rest. I can truly say it's one of my most memorable hunts ever.

My mind was focused more on poison rather than hunting back on October 1, 2011. As I sat on the ground, I just imagined all the chemicals flowing through my legs, arms, and body. *I probably have more chemotherapy in my body than blood,*

I thought. Earlier in the week, nurses were filling my veins with chemo. I was so weak and fatigued, I barely had enough strength to carry my rifle. Chemo does all kinds of weird things to your body. However, chronic fatigue may be the biggest side effect. On this morning, I managed enough energy to hunt at one of my favorite places. Once at the right spot, I rested comfortably against a tall pine with plenty of longleaf pine needles underneath me.

This wasn't an early morning hunt either. I woke from my night's sleep around 8:30 am. So, the hunt began around 10:00 AM, probably the time most hunters have called it a morning. From experience, I know mid-morning is a fantastic time to hunt. I truly believe big bucks move more consistently in the later morning hours than any other time of day. This hunt was about to prove my theory.

The first thirty minutes of my hunt was great resting time. Nothing was moving either. I opened my eyes just enough to check the corn pile and then rest some more. Well, at the 10:30 corn pile check, I saw something off to the left. *Holy cow... it's a big buck!* I saw a nice eight-point heading right toward the corn pile. He walked right up and started eating like an old bull. I eased the rifle up and watched him for a while. He was standing broadside probably no further than sixty yards. The deer didn't have a care in the world. Yes, I had the rifle, but my killing instinct wasn't with me today. I picked up the camera and did my best to get a good photo. He would be the biggest buck that I had ever photographed. The deer posed for several minutes and finally walked off. A pine tree kept blurring my photo. However, it ended up looking fairly decent. After he walked off, I decided to head back home. I was so happy to see him, but I had no desire to shoot this buck. He was lucky. Hopefully, he lived a good life. I sure would like to see some of his children on a hunt soon!

The Lucky Chemo Buck

TOUGHNESS

I really do wish I had some sort of grand tale to share. You know what I mean. Let me tell you about my Heisman Trophy or the story of hitting the walk-off homerun that won the national championship game. How about the time I saved us from the bear? It's sad to say, but I have nothing that exciting. However, I do have a few that are extreme in their own way.

One afternoon, my wife (Lisa) and I were in the kitchen talking and laughing. The day before, my son hit a line drive and her eye socket was the glove. She ended up going to the hospital for examination. Thankfully, a bruised and sore eye was the only outcome. I said to her in the kitchen, "Now, can you imagine getting shot in the face like Daddy did?" Of course, she said no. Over the next few minutes, I dug way back into my memory bank trying to relive that miserable experience.

This shooting accident happened when I was eight years old. C.J. was quail hunting with some friends and a guest. Before the hunt even began, C.J immediately questioned his father about the hunting skills of the guest. The guest was an inexperienced hunter. We call them green horns. Quail hunting in the South used to be a big deal. It was a time for close friends to enjoy a day outdoors together as much as anything. Close friends also meant experienced hunters. This is very important while quail hunting because the hunters have to trust those around them. Both hunters and birds can be in close proximity to each other during a hunt. A covey getting up can cause a less experienced hunter to get excited and lose focus on his surroundings. Well, that's exactly what happened on this hunt in 1984. The guest, a DOCTOR, shot into the covey and hit C.J. in the face with number eights (birdshot), the size of shot used in the shotgun shells for bird hunting. This all unfolded on a typical school day for me. I found out the details after school. The next time I saw him he was bandaged up in the Orangeburg Hospital. I don't remember how much pain he felt, but I do recall everyone not knowing whether he would see again. Also, the pellets to this day are still in the side of his face and ear. Luckily, he did not lose sight in his eye. However, he has had to wear glasses ever since the accident and has visited the eye doctor many, many times. How about that for a day of quail hunting?

Here's another story about C.J. many don't know. We were surf fishing in Beaufort one fall day. Our favorite spot was off the front of Caper's Island. Thinking back on how this was accomplished boggles my mind. Not the fishing part, but how we arrived at the fishing hole. This is going to be hard to explain, but I'm going to do my best. The front of Caper's Island is a beach. It's simply white sand and breakers pounding the surf like any South Carolina beach. It's also undeveloped. Back in the eighties, there was a small creek that fed into the island. The only way to get to this creek was from the front beach. This meant battling the breakers. Our small, fourteen-foot john boat with a twenty-five horsepower Johnson was basically turned into a redneck surfboard. We would haul tail toward the beach and catch the right wave. Then we would ride it until we were in the mouth of the creek. Once safely in the mouth, we would jump out of the boat and push it into the creek. This was a critical moment, because if you didn't push fast enough a wave could break over the back of the boat and fill it with water. Thankfully, this never happened that I can remember. Once in the creek, the boat was protected from the rough breakers.

After anchoring the boat: it was time to wade back into the surf and catch fish. Most days we did very well. However, the story I'm about to share all but ended my surf fishing days. In all honesty, C.J. and his buddies would do anything to catch fish. I don't know of anyone else who arrived at a fishing hole this way. It's a little crazy. Well, on this particular day, I was tired of fishing. A twelve-year-old just can't handle much surf fishing. The waves are constantly pounding against you. After enough fishing, I would take a fish that I caught and play with it in a tidal pool. I loved watching them swim around. C.J. only stopped fishing when it was time to go. However, there was one catfish who got revenge for all caught fish.

Here's what happened. It occurred on a typical bite. Nothing out of the ordinary, until an unlikely event took place just before handling the fish. While reaching for his catch, a wave caught the fish, and sort of threw it towards C.J.'s face. Out of self-defense, he threw his hand up toward his face to block the fish. In case you don't know, catfish have spines for pectoral fins. Their dorsal fin is also a single spine. All three are roughly one inch long and very sharp. Saltwater catfish also have some type of poison on their spines. A saltwater catfish sticking into your hand hurts ten times worse than their freshwater cousins. Well, one of the pectoral fins punctured the skin on C.J.'s hand between his thumb and index finger. When I say punctured, I mean it went all the way through the muscle in between the two fingers. Somehow, he pulled the fish out of his hand and walked back toward the boat. To this day, I can remember hearing him say, "I'm about to faint." I didn't know what to do. He sat down in the boat while putting a bag of ice on the back of his neck. After some time passed, we packed everything up and started home. I have no idea how we managed to get the boat back through the breakers, but we did. This was my first time navigating the boat all the way to the landing with little to no help. He could barely hold his head up from the pain. I was a very experienced twelve-year-old on the water, but I'm sure I wasn't ready for this challenge. Surf fishing nowadays doesn't require an amphibious assault tactic. I'll always remember that little catfish.

I have one more fishing story about C.J. This story boils down to a combination of many errors. First of all, we should have never gone fishing. Somehow two experienced fishermen felt like we could catch fish while a tropical depression moved along the coast. We agreed fish could be caught—needed to be caught—in this storm. I still don't know what we were thinking.

Well, this fishing day was about to turn into a memorable trip for all the wrong reasons. Our day began at low tide, and the chop on the water was very rough as you can imagine. From the get-go, our day consisted of battling a twenty-mile-per-hour west wind. We fished out of my flats boat, so I was at the helm navigating. C.J. sat on the front deck facing toward me, his back toward the water. That was a huge mistake... not only in hindsight, but in basic boating safety. He had nothing to brace on in case we hit something. Crab pots, lumber, and sandbars are common in the ocean. Of course, as many times as we have been on the water, nothing could phase us. But on this day, it did. The chop hindered my ability to see a sandbar that I have safely maneuvered around hundreds of times. It was approximately six inches beneath the water. While making a right turn towards our fishing hole, I ran us head on into the sandbar. We were probably going 10-15 mph, which isn't very fast, but a decent speed for rough water. I have hit them harder before but not with someone on the front deck. I endured the sudden stop with no problem, but C.J. didn't. He flipped out of the boat onto the sandbar. It scared the mess out of me. I jumped out of the boat to help him up. All I saw was blood running from his head. He had a two-inch gash on it because his head was cut by the bow cleat. It looked horrible. I instantly knew stitches would be necessary. The bleeding slowed after applying pressure and ice for a while. My thoughts now turned to finding a hospital. This was a short-lived task. Once his cobwebs were cleared, he said, "We might as well go fishing. We drove all the way here and have plenty of bait. Let's just go fishing." He has always been the boss, so we headed to the hole and fished.

After about five minutes, however, I couldn't take it. I said, "This is stupid, let's go!" A couple hours later, we arrived at the Barnwell hospital. He needed about ten stitches to close his cut. I wish that was the end of the story. X-rays showed he also chipped a piece of bone off of a vertebra. Thankfully, it broke in such a way that it didn't require surgery. Time would heal this injury without any lasting issues. So, it's an absolute fact: the man fished with a broken neck and a bloody gash on his head. I really don't know what category to put this in. Is it tough as hell or plain crazy? All I know is fishing is serious business in our family.

DEER GETS HUNTER

D enmark, SC. has great deer hunting. I truly believe it has improved over the past thirty years. Our habitat is perfect for supporting large numbers of deer. Denmark is still very rural with a decent amount of farming. So, with all of the great habitat and farming surrounding the town, why in the world would a buck ever hang around downtown? He got confused... that's all I can say. He must have preferred the small-town life.

While flipping through an old scrapbook recently, I saw a newspaper clipping from many years ago. It was the picture of a small six-point buck that got lost in Denmark. The caption mentions how the deer was spotted running around in the horse pasture of Clifford Ray, Sr. This was my Granddaddy's horse pasture, which was right next to the Fire Department. The buck figured out this wasn't the place to be and obviously decided to find another spot to roam. He then ran across town. This journey was probably one-half mile or so. There are no details of the buck's trip though the town, but I do know where he ended up. The buck jumped into Clifford Ray, Jr.'s truck windshield as he was driving into town. The collision killed the buck. C.J. was injured as well. During the impact of the deer coming through the windshield, the steering column was broken. Through self-defense, C.J. somehow managed to protect himself from the oncoming buck. However, during this exchange, several ribs were cracked. Now that's a father-son deer drive worth remembering.

Out of all the big bucks killed by C.J., this one little six-point makes the local paper. Now, that just doesn't seem right. It's time to bring back to life some of the pictures that have been tucked away in photo albums for years. I picked out some of the best photos. Back then, no one took the time to make a hunting photo look the best it could be. The deer were just thrown into the back of the truck with tools, beer cans, and buckets. Here are a few that are presentable. Trust me, this represents the very tip of the iceberg. Several hundred have been loaded into the back of pick-ups over the years. I know it sounds like an exaggeration, but it's the truth.

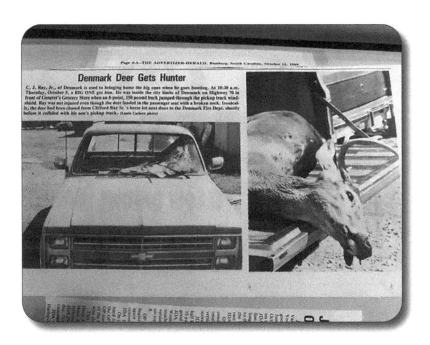

The City Slicker Buck

FISHING ELECTRICITY

I seldom share this story with anyone. I'm afraid it might fall into the category of a Bigfoot or UFO sighting. I hope I'm not that crazy! Well, in all honesty, my friend standing a few feet away had a hard time believing me. He witnessed the entire thing! It basically blew me away, too! You know what, that's a bad choice of words. It almost blew me away.

"Well, what did you catch today?" asked my buddy, Cholly Parker, over the phone. He enjoys an update after all of my fishing trips. Cholly receives the honest, unexaggerated version. Then once the facts are mulled over, we might put a stretched version of the truth out there for others to hear. I'm just saying… we like to make others laugh. My reply to the original question was this: "Are you sitting down?"

"Oh my! You caught a whale!" was his enthusiastic response.

"Not today. It's better than that." I laughed and began a story beyond belief. "We caught one small spottail, a sting ray about three-feet wide, a seagull, and I got struck by lightning."

Cholly replied, "That's gonna be a tough trip to top. I need to hear more!"

Ben and I arrived at Steamboat Landing just as the sun was rising on a Saturday morning in September. We were both excited about our day of tarpon fishing. I hopped out of the truck, and Ben started backing the boat down the ramp. That's when a major warning sign halted our progress. I could see dark storm clouds off in the distance, exactly where we wanted to fish. However, it didn't seem that bad, but within a matter of seconds, we both saw a violent bolt of lightning. This storm announced its presence with authority. No discussion was necessary; we had to wait until the storm passed. While killing time, we planned our day and made fun of the idiot fishing off of the metal dock at the landing. How dumb can you be fishing on a metal dock when lightning is around? I even turned to Ben and commented, "This fellow is about to be crab bait once lightning strikes him!" We both just laughed and continued to watch the lightning off in the distance, five-plus miles away. Little did we know business was about to pick up!

All of a sudden, it looked like someone flipped a light switch on at the landing and the entire place lit up. We both heard the spooky, crackling sound of lighting and a gigantic *BOOM* exploded near us. It felt like the whole area shook and the hairs started standing up on my body! This entire event unfolded in less than a second. Well, while all this was taking place, something was grabbing me around my ankles. In between the crackling and the boom, ground level current (lightning) had my body handcuffed. That's the best way I can explain what happened. It felt like some type of force had lassoed my ankles together. My entire body felt weird. Had I not been leaning on the boat, I know for a fact that I would have fallen over. I felt no pain, just a weird energy in my body. My initial comment to Ben was, "I just got struck by lightning!" Immediately, we both sprinted to the truck for safety. Ben didn't believe me at first, but after my animated explanation, he came around. It was hard for me to believe, too. While sitting in the truck, my body felt strange for a minute or two. It felt like I was full of electricity. Ben and I both know we dodged a big one! Even the fellow on the dock ran. He looked like a spooked cat running past us!

I'm here to tell you from this single experience that we are worth absolutely nothing to mother nature. Had that bolt of lightning it me, I would have been blown to a million pieces all over that salt marsh. The fiddler crabs would have had a wonderful time filling their bellies. That's a fact. There are no words to describe the feeling of helplessness during that one second. All Ben and I could do was close our eyes and pray it wasn't our time to die. Shoot, we didn't even have time for that.

After the dust had settled and the storm cleared, there was only one thing to do. It was time to fish. By 8:00 am we were fishing where the storm had passed. Of course, my internal thoughts were running wild. I couldn't believe, figure out, or comprehend the early morning event. We survived! It simply wasn't my day or Ben's to clock out. Two fishing fools lived to fish another day. It was probably fitting the first thing we caught was a seagull. You know what? A seagull is pretty common for me. When I catch a mermaid, that's when I'll know for certain that the fishing gods have chosen me. For whatever reason, I'm still around to share many more tales. Who wants to go fishing with me? We might just hook that mermaid!

Seagull Catch & Release

SECOND CHANCE

I was either going to love deer hunting or hate it. It was my choice. I just happened to grow up with someone who hunted every free moment possible. When deer season came in, no one asked what C.J. was doing. Everyone knew he was in the woods waiting on a buck. I can remember, as a little boy, being mad at him if he came home from an afternoon hunt without a deer. In order to satisfy my high demand and our love of hunting, he usually ended up with thirty to forty deer per season. You need to understand, hunting was different forty years ago in the South Carolina low country. At that time, hunters usually shot the first buck that stepped out. No one cared about quality bucks, spread limits, or anything that had to do with deer management. It was a just different time and era. Further, we ran a farm at that time. Not only did the hunting help to protect our crops, but farm hands counted on us to help provide them with free meat to feed their families.

You would think, being around so much hunting, that it would be easy. Well, it was the exact opposite when I was a youngster. Time after time, I somehow let big bucks slip through my grasp. It was so frustrating having to explain over and over again how I messed up. I just couldn't find a cure for Buck Fever. My nerves always got the best of me. Those bucks had to see the entire tree top shaking. Also, I simply had to learn how to hunt on my own.

I remember my first hunt like it was yesterday. It took place on a sunny Sunday afternoon. I hunted out of a ten-foot high wooden box stand. A cut-up burlap sack placed around the outside was the camouflage. My La-Z-Boy chair was a five-gallon bucket. We were high-tech hunters. Once situated in the stand, my focus had nothing to do with hunting. The cherry sucker in my pocket was a priority, the one with the bubble gum in the center. I loved those things back then and still do. Well, while engrossed with the sucker, a nice buck walked out of the woods from my left. He headed directly to the corn pile. I'm telling you this all happened in no time. Yes, even before I got to the bubble gum part. Next thing I knew, he was broadside with his head down in the corn pile. Hunting is easy! All I remember next was picking up the 30-30 with iron sights (no scope) and doing my best to make a good shot. I pulled the trigger, expecting a loud bang and a dead buck. Disappointment soon set in. All I heard was a click. My big buck heard it too. He took off just like he was hit.

I forgot to load the gun! Talk about going from excitement to the absolute pit of disgust in two seconds. This was the first screw up of many over my first couple of years hunting.

Just a few weeks later, I was able to see the sucker buck. C.J. killed him. I remembered what his rack looked like the few moments he was in my presence. It was a nice nine point. This just made me sick. That was supposed to be my first buck. Lesson number one learned: load the gun after sitting down. Lesson number two was just around the corner for this young hunter.

As deer season progresses, so does the opportunity of killing a big one. There is a special time every season that all hunters look forward too. It's called: the rut. Bucks just lose their minds during this period of the year. This is a time when even an inexperienced hunter can claim a monster. I'm living proof to most of that statement. My first encounter with a rutting monster left a scar that still bothers me some thirty years later.

The scene was the very same stand that I failed on my first hunt. The only difference was this hunt took place on a Saturday morning. It was a cold, blue-skied morning and the leaves were falling all around me. After an hour or so of silence, the woods to my right just exploded with activity. Being such a young hunter, I didn't understand what was happening. A doe shot out of the woods. She was running wide open and bolted across the small clearing which was surrounded by hardwoods. Within seconds, the biggest buck that I had ever seen came from the very same spot. He looked like he had antlers going every direction. It was incredible. The image has been burned into my memory. Well, I somehow managed to throw up the rifle and fire off a quick shot in his direction. He never broke stride. That was not good news. This inexperienced hunter was quickly becoming an expert on how bucks react after being missed. Within seconds, another buck ran right out of the hardwoods and stopped directly in front of me. *Bam*! He dropped dead. It was a consolation prize. I was still happy that I got one, but since that day, I can still see the image of that monster buck running across the clearing.

This missed buck has haunted me for years. Many, many times, I have wished for just one more chance to make amends. Mulligans and big bucks do not go together. I can say that with confidence. However, I do believe the hunting gods offered me another opportunity to redeem myself. I'm forty-four now, and the biggest miss happened when I was thirteen. It just took three decades for that second chance. Just a few weeks ago, many childhood failures were almost instantly forgiven by a special buck.

Over thirty years, the wooden box stand that I made so many missing memories in my youth has rotten and fallen over. The cow pasture (mentioned in the "Monsters" chapter) that I crossed to get to the stand has now been planted in pines. The pines are nearly twenty-five-feet tall. Time sure does fly by. Now the planted pines are where I sit, facing toward the old box stand. The clearing does remain, where the big buck bolted across. However, the main focus of my hunts now is the fire lane which runs between planted pines and hardwoods. Scrapes and rubs are everywhere along the lane. Also, a corn pile adds extra incentive for the deer to come in my direction.

Well, the stars aligned on October 4, 2020; a day that will bring a smile to my face forever. It was a great day for hunting, but a full moon was hurting productivity. Deer generally prefer to move under the bright moon light and rest during the morning hours. Their activity then picks up mid-afternoon and they return to cover before an afternoon hunt typically begins. My hunting day was following this exact pattern. Of course, this is not set in stone as you are about to discover.

I didn't see a deer all morning, and two hours into the afternoon hunt proved to be just as empty. However, business picked up around 6:30 PM. The quick glimpse of a deer got me excited. I just happened to see the deer for one second in the old clearing where I once hunted. Experience led me to believe that the body of the deer was a buck, but I couldn't make out antlers, and my quick glimpse was all I had. I looked hard for him over several minutes and did not see the deer again. I figured he veered off in another direction. Luck was on my side this afternoon, though.

He walked right out of the hardwoods and crossed the fire lane about two-hundred yards off to my right. At this moment, he was still sort of facing me, just off at an angle (about forty-five degrees). The buck was leaving the thick woods and making way into the pines. All I could see was his huge rack. I am a ground hunter and knew that a potential one-hundred yard shot off my knee wasn't practical. I quickly swirled around to use my back rest (a pine tree) as a rifle rest. Many trees were in between the two of us, blocking my movement. I'm telling you, it was agonizing waiting on him to come into clear view. I knew at any moment he could veer off track and leave me empty handed. Today was my day. He did everything I needed to get a clear shot. Once in my lane, I shot quickly because he never stopped walking. I knew the crosshairs were on him.

I saw his tail flip straight up in the air, and it appeared he bolted back in the general direction he came from. The shot felt good, but his exit lacked something to be desired in my opinion.

Let's go look for some blood. My eagerness to find blood was met with a gut-wrenching observation. I couldn't find a single drop, nor even a hair. *Oh no! I know I didn't miss this buck.* So, the search for the buck began with no promise at all. I'm already behind the eight ball. I looked and looked with no luck. After about ten minutes, I double checked the area where blood should have been. *Absolutely Nothing!* By this time, I was losing hope. I decided to head into the woods at the exact location of where he came from. Each step deeper into the woods caused my hope to lessen. I saw no signs of a wounded deer. *How did this happen?* All hope was soon lost as another blown opportunity became a bitter reality. I paused about one hundred yards into the woods to gather my thoughts. After a minute or two, I decided to walk up through the old clearing and head back home. My very next step set off a fury of hunting excitement. The buck jumped about twenty yards in front of me. He was scrambling to get away even with a severely hurt hip. All I could see was his huge rack putting distance in between us.

This buck is not getting away from me!

I immediately started running after him. I quickly realized he was much faster than me, even with a .270 bullet in his hip. A kill shot was my best option. I stopped chasing and he eventually stopped running as well. Bushes and briars separated us. I found him in my scope and fired. His head lowered and I cautiously approached him. Once within a few feet, I began admiring an incredible animal. *Holy cow,* I thought, *it's a ten-point!*

What a memory to go along with my biggest miss in basically the same stand. I have never chased one down like this before. It was quite a thrill coming out on the winning side. I can honestly say this buck looks like the twin of the one I missed thirty years ago. This was the perfect way to come full circle with the one that got away.

The Second Chance 10 point

Bucknell Football 2018

I'm veering off course with this one. This story has nothing to do with hunting or fishing. The message means a great deal to me, and I feel like it needs to be shared.

In 2018, my family traveled all the way to the Little League World Series in Williamsport, Pennsylvania. Like many, I have watched this annually on television and only dreamed of attending in person. I can now strike this one off the bucket-list.

It was fantastic. This is definitely an event that's even better in person than on television. You can't beat the ticket prices either. The games are all free! It's first come first serve. Some games have plenty of available seats. However, others fill up within a matter of minutes. It's a mad scramble to find a seat. We were a part of this scramble one evening. Harrison did an outstanding job finding us two third-base seats for the Hawaii-Georgia game. This was the prime-time game on a Friday night, a game that ended up being a classic. Hawaii won 3-0. The game went eleven innings and was tied for the longest game in Little League World Series history.

Well, I could go on and on about the World Series. However, this isn't the main subject of this story. Our family also loves football. Exploring college football stadiums is one of our favorite hobbies. Vacations are often built around a new stadium that we can explore. All I can say is, don't leave a stadium door open or we will find it.

Bucknell University is very close to South Williamsport. The morning of our second day at the World Series, we spent time admiring Bucknell's stadium. The boys ran the field, rolled on the grass, and looked for treasures. They found things like used mouthpieces, towels, water bottles, and wristbands. These items are more prized than pieces of gold. Yes, we let them keep the mouthpieces. My wife and I looked around the stadium, took a lot of pictures, and thought of ways to make the most of our football experience.

Since fall practice was in full swing, Lisa had a great idea. She found the football office phone number in the press box (the door was open) and called it. Just maybe, the boys could meet the head coach. You never know until you try. The answer is always no if you don't ask. Luck was on our side that day; the team was scheduled to practice at 10:30 AM. All we had to do was wait one hour in order to meet the coach and the team.

Right on time, the team and coaches made their way onto the field. Head Coach Joe Susan greeted us immediately. He treated Harrison and Jace like they were his top recruits. Our quick two-minute visit turned into ninety minutes of football. The boys met the players, Coach Susan gave them a signed game-ball, and we were invited to watch practice. It was a special morning for the Ray family. Coach truly gave us a top-notch experience. You know, successful coaches have a way of winning people over. I guess it's called recruiting. I'm telling you, we were in football heaven.

Coach Susan also added us to his email list the day of our visit. Periodically, he would email out a document of wisdom gained from his coaching experience. Receiving emails from Coach Susan was always a welcomed treasure for me. I printed and filed every wisdom email. One story included a quote from Theodore Roosevelt. It's exceptional, in my opinion. See what you think:

> "It is not the critic that counts, not the man who points out how the strong man stumbled or where the doer of deeds could have done better. The credit belongs to the man who is actually in the arena; whose face is marred by the dust and sweat and blood; who strives valiantly, who errs and often comes up short again and again; who knows the great enthusiasms, the great

devotions and spends himself in a worthy cause; who, at best, knows in the end triumph of high achievement, and who at worst, if he fails, at least fails while daring greatly, so that his place shall never be with those cold and timid souls. Who know neither victory nor defeat."

I'm glad Lisa opened the press box door. This was a special morning for the entire family, a morning that was capped off by an afternoon of baseball at one of the world's most famous venues. This was simply an amazing day: August 17, 2018.

The Boys with Head Coach Joe Susan

The Boys with the Quarterbacks

MEAN DEAN

I missed my battle with Blackbeard. We should have met on the high seas and fought for the gold and girl. Winner take all, that's how it should have been. Two pirates fighting a battle that would be talked about for centuries. Of course, my name in the history books would go down as Mean Dean—a name earned through battle, not just given. I would've been the meanest pirate to sail on the North Atlantic. A Mean Dean Jolly Roger flying high above the mast meant doom for any challenging captain. Word would have spread quickly to all seagoing vessels about my reputation. Of course, all vessels deserved a chance to wave the white flag. Your ship and men would be spared for the right price. However, refusal to meet demands would be a grave decision.

All of this has a great ring to it. This is how the history books should remember a tough pirate. However, Blackbeard is the one who made history as the world's most famous pirate, not Mean Dean. For whatever reason, my desire to rule the North Atlantic as Blackbeard did will most likely never come true. As I write this story, I'm still searching for my high seas adventure. I hope I haven't missed my ship. My Jolly Roger is flying high, so look out! The dream lives on.

You know what? Maybe, in a way, I have missed my ship. My dream job would have been to work on some type of boat. I would have loved to operate a tugboat or any type of working vessel. Not just work on the boat, but be the captain—the person with all the answers, who everyone trusted and counted on. I don't know why, but this type of opportunity never even crossed my path. I'm a landlocked seaman. Thankfully, a lifetime of fishing has soothed my internal disappointment. Navigating my flats boat along the coast of South Carolina brings great joy to me. A few hundred years ago, pirates sailed the very same waters I am fishing on today. I think that's pretty neat.

I often wonder why a career on the water never materialized for me. What could I have done differently? I often kick myself for not searching with more conviction. Now common sense reveals that I should have gone to the ports and shipyards along the coast and just asked. I just needed to get my foot in the door and then work my way up. However, the risk wasn't taken. My lack of getting after it frustrates me to some degree now. My dreams simply faded away, completely unfulfilled. I'm starting to think, had Blackbeard and I faced off, he would have beaten my butt!

Now it's time to shift gears a little and dive deeper into the words above. The introduction will begin to come alive. In order to accomplish this, I need to share a story my preacher told one Sunday morning in church. This will illustrate my real-life situation. It's a fictional story that became all too real.

Three trees were talking to each other in the forest. The first tree said to the others, "When they cut me down, I want my lumber to be made into a huge ship that carries a king across oceans." The second tree chimed in and said, "When I'm cut down, I want my wood to be made into columns of a gigantic castle for the most powerful ruler in all the land." The third tree stated, "When I'm cut down, I want to be made into the most gorgeous bed for a king."

Soon all three were cut down. The tree that dreamed of being a ship was made into a small fishing boat. The second tree that wanted to be made into the columns of a castle ended up being cut into posts and thrown into a pile at the lumber yard. The third tree was made into a feed trough for farm animals. All three trees were disappointed, as their dreams went unfulfilled.

As always, time began to pass and the future seemed fruitless. Then one day, the little fishing boat was needed by a man who needed to escape the crowd. This little boat allowed Jesus to better preach to the large crowd that had gathered on the shore. The second tree wanted to be columns of a castle for the most powerful ruler in all the land; well, those posts were made into the cross that held Jesus during His death. Finally, the feed trough was turned into a manger where the King of Kings lay at His birth. The moral of the story is this: The Lord will use you how He best sees fit, and at the appropriate time. He will see that your heart's desire is exceeded.

Now, what does this have to do with my dreams and frustration of not working on the water? I'm about to explain with another church story. I couldn't believe my ears as the preacher shared another lesson a few weeks after telling the tree story. This is retold to the best of my ability:

Have you ever taken a close look at the ceiling of our sanctuary? Our ceiling is shaped like the bottom of a ship. It's almost identical to an upside-down ship. The area where you are sitting is called the "nave". This word comes from the Latin word "navis" for *ship*, and was meant to portray the reality that the church is a ship. Navis is where we get our word *navy*. The sea, in our case, is the world outside our walls. Just as people are safe on a ship from the sea, people come inside our doors to find protection or guidance to withstand the outside world. We are here to get people through the storms of life.

Here's the final piece of this illustration. Currently, I am the facilities manager for a large church in my hometown. By accepting this position, I ended a four-year search to satisfy an internal push. It was so strong I couldn't ignore it. The feeling was driving me crazy at my previous job. Something kept forcing me to look for a different place to work. Trust me, working at a church was never on my radar. Taking the church job was a risk. My current job was great and allowed me to be outdoors all day long. I loved that aspect. So why in the world was the church the place for me?

Unbeknownst to me, this is where I would have the opportunity to work on and manage a large ship! Instead of battling Blackbeard, I am doing my part to keep us running (or sailing) in order to battle the evil forces of this world. I do believe the Lord put me here for a reason. I'm a living example of the tree illustration that came true. How about that!

Maybe what I just wrote about was orchestrated by the Lord. I'm sure not smart enough to think of it on my own. It's mighty strange how I was able to find a job that satisfied my mariner desire. I do believe I'm being used in a more meaningful manner than my original intentions. I bet the trees did, too.

Finally, there's a reason for ending the book with this story. I simply wanted to close in the same manner that I try to end each day. Psalm 127:1 says, "Unless the Lord builds a house, the work of the builders is wasted. Unless the Lord protects a city, guarding it with sentries will do no good." I try my best every night to study the Bible. The wisdom gained pays dividends each day. This entire book is my little way of doing my part. The Bible says to let your light shine. I know without the Lord's guidance and help my efforts would be a total waste. I hope someone, somewhere, someday, enjoys these stories.

CONCLUSION

I remember the last phone call with Captain Rick. He shared with me some incredible numbers. I was at work during this phone call. I should have scribbled the numbers down. It just wasn't a top priority at the time. My thoughts were consumed over his cancer battle. However, here is what he said. This is to the best of my memory, and I'm not off by much. In 2020, after only eight months of fishing, Captain Rick's charters caught over 3,000 fish, the majority being redfish (with a total close to 1,800). The rest of the catch included trout, black drum, flounder, and a few other species. Just so you know, charter vessels are required to keep an accurate count of the fish caught per trip. This number is then submitted to the South Carolina Department of Natural Resources on a monthly basis. His number was dead on. I know how in tune he was on those trips.

Captain Rick had over three-hundred named fishing drops (fishing holes). I mentioned to him during one of our trips together, "You need to document all those spots one day. People would love to have a guide's secrets." He laughed. After a short conversation, we both agreed it would be a huge undertaking to locate on a map and detail each drop.

He spent over twenty years searching and fine tuning his charter business. The fishing advice and knowledge he passed on to his fellow friends is priceless. That's one big reason I enjoyed spending time with Rick. His willingness to help a person catch more fish was a gift. That's the type of man he was. He easily made friends for life. That's a trait worth more than gold. His love of fishing will live forever through everyone he touched. Anyone lucky enough to know Rick would agree.

One of my personal goals was to hand Captain Rick a copy of this book. I wanted to see and hear his excitement once it was in his hand. Sadly, cancer didn't allow that to happen.

Rick's cancer journey has added fuel to my fire. It makes me hate cancer even more. It reminds me to live the best life possible. We can't all catch 3,000 fish in eight months, but we can all enjoy every single fish we catch. Captain Rick Percy sure did. That's the *Happy Outdoors* attitude.

The End

Captain Rick Promoting his Book

ABOUT THE AUTHOR

C lifford Jardine Ray III (Dean) grew up in Denmark, South Carolina. He was blessed from day one to live on the family farm. The farm offered him unlimited hunting opportunities and free time in the outdoors. Dean graduated from Clemson University with a degree in Wildlife and Fisheries Biology. He now lives in Beech Island, South Carolina with his wife, Lisa, and their two boys. When the boys aren't playing sports, you can often find the family swimming on the Edisto River.

The Ray Family